Quadratic Formula
by Thomas Nguyen

Oh Quadratic formula, you are so useful,
Especially when there is a quadratic equation
That I cannot factor.
With the discriminant underneath the square root,
I can determine how manny X intercepts it has.
My professor told me that you were derived from completing the square.
Let me tell you something,
I want to be your b squared minus 4ac.
I want to be your discriminant

Trouble with Fractions

by Thomas Nguyen

When i began Grade 7 at the beginning of the school year, we had to learn fractions. I found them so confusing, especially the common denominator part. I find fractions difficult. Mr. McDonald, my math teacher is a terrible teacher. He doesn't even take time to explain things.

When I don't get something, he expects us to look at our textbooks. Luckily, I have smart kids in my class to helpmeet out. After school, I spend lots of time at their houses getting help from them.

When I was just learning how to add fractions, I found it hard to add fractions with different denominators.

Okay Travis," Joe said. "Let's look at Question 7 on Pg. 20 of the work book."

As I looked at the question, I asked him, "How do we find the common denominator?"

"Okay, so you have to add 5/3 to 7/8. So, the common denominator will be 24 because both 3 and 8 go into 24."

Next, I asked joe how I could get both fractions to the common denominator. He told me to multiply 5/3 by 8 on both the top and bottom and 7/8 by 3 on the top and bottom in order to get both fractions to the same denominator.

"Remember Travis, what you do to the numerator, you gotta do to the denominator," Joe explained.

I started to get those annoying fractions and they became less difficult the more I practiced them. Joe would check my work and make sure that my solutions and answers were correct. I started to get it. Adding fractions with different denominators wasn't so bad after all.

Numerator and Denominator

by Thomas Nguyen

You are my numerator, and I am your denominator.

I just cannot equal to zero,

Because that will make the fraction undefined.

The fraction is indeterminate when we are both zero.

We must take it to the limit.

Will the limit go to positive or negative infinity?

Will it go to a finite number?

Our puzzle must be solved.

Math Jokes

by Thomas Nguyen

1 Why is a pie called a pie? 3.14.

2 What is Christian times Christian? Christian squared.

3 A boy is going to Math camp with his buddy. One time the boy yelled, "Outch!) His buddy asks, "Are you okay?" The boy replies, "I sat on my compass!" His buddy says, "At least you will be able to measure the angle of the scar."

4. Charles got out of bed. His mom asked, "What would you like to eat today?" Charles replied, "I would like to have three squared meals a day".

5. George was minding his own business, when he heard his mom call him.

"George, I need to talk to you about something! It's about your credit card bill!"

"What is it mom?" George asked.

"You have a balance of negative four-thousand dollars"

"Oh snap! How am I going to get the money to pay it back?"

6. What did 1/8 say to 1/3 about the number 24? I believe that

we have a common denominator.

7. What did one line on the graph say to the perpendicular line?

See you at the intersection.

8. What did the algebra equation say to the math professor?

Find my X.

9. What did Sine over Cosine say to Cosine over Sine? Hello

my little cotangent.6

10. What did the quadratic equation say to the linear equation?

    Nice slope.

11. What did the numerator say to the denominator? You can be

    anything except 0.

12. What did Pi say to negative 4? Stop being so negative.

Math

by Thomas Nguyen

Mr. Newby: Hello class, today, we are going to learn integers. We are going to learn how to add them. A positive plus a positive is a positive. For example Positive three plus positive seven is positive 10. A negative plus a negative is a negative. When you add a positive and a negative, you have to subtract and take the sign of the bigger number. For example negative fifteen plus positive 9 equals negative six.

Josh: So, fifteen is bigger than nine?

Mr. Newby: You are correct Josh. Can anyone tell me what positive fifteen plus positive ten is? (Ashley raises her hand.) Ashley.

Ashley: positive twenty-five.

Mr. Newby: Yes, that is right. Can anyone tell me what negative eleven plus negative thirteen is? (Lily raises her hand.) Lily.

Lily: Negative twenty-four.

Mr. Newby: Correct! Now, can anyone tell me what negative twenty seven plus negative eight is? (Annie raises her hand.) Annie.

Annie: Negative twenty-eight.

Mr. Newby: I'm sorry Annie, the answer is incorrect. (Can anyone tell me what the correct answer for this question is? (Josh raises his hand.) Josh.

Josh: Negative thirty-five.

Mr. Newby: You are correct Josh.

Annie: Mr. Newby, I am terrible at math.

Mr. Newby: Why do you say that?

Annie: It's because my brain is so mathless. I can't even calculate numbers correctly.

Mr. Newby: What is sixteen times four?

Annie: ninety-seven.

Mr. Newby: That is not the answer. How can it be ninety-seven?

Annie: (Crying.) See, I am so bad at math!

Mr. Newby: You need to calm down. I'll help you figure this question and your classmates will help youtoo. (Mr. Newby writes on the board.) First, we must multiply the ones. What is six times four?

too. (Mr. Newby writes on the board.) First, we must multiply the ones. What is six times four?

Annie: (Hesatating.) Twenty-four?

Mr. Newby: Yes! Now, what is ten times four?

Annie: forty.

Mr. Newby: Correcto! Now, what is forty plus twenty-four?

Annie: (Figuring out the answer as she writes her calculations on paper.) Sixty-four!

Mr. Newby: That is the answer!

Annie: Really? I figured it out?

Mr. Newby: Yes you did. See, you're not terrible at math! You just need to have confidence in yourself.

Little Professor
by Thomas Nguyen

Hello, my name is James and I am in Grade 8. My favourite subjects are math and science. My favourite sciences are chemistry and physics. I can do math up to Grade 10 and my math teacher, Mr. Barns is impressed. However, My Language Arts teacher, Mrs. Klein, does not like math. I'm not even allowed to do math in her class and that is sad.

I have three other friends, John, Liz, and Allen, who also are math geeks. They also like physics, just like I do. All the other kids call us "little professors". We've been called "nerds" in Grade 7.

Today, I'm going to tell you the time we got our math and physics books taken away. It was October of our Grade 8 year. Everyone else was silently reading while my three friends and I sat at the back of Mrs. Klein's class doing trig. All the other kids looked at us with weird looks.

"What is this?" a boy with a hockey shirt asked, pointing to me.

"Trig," I said.

I tried to explain what trig was, but he didn't get it. All of a sudden, Mrs. Klein caught John, Liz, and Allen doing math.

"Guys, you're supposed to be reading, not doing math," she said.

"We are reading, technically. We are problem solving at the same time," John said trying to sound smart.

"There is no math allowed in my class. This is Language Arts, not math class."

After Mrs. Klein walked away from us, we went back to doing trig again. Ten minutes later, she took our math books away and gave us a novel to read instead. After Language Arts was over, we told the math teacher what happened. He felt sorry for us. But at the same time, he told us, "When you want to do math, wait until it's math class."

Our math teacher let's us do trig in his class. He was really impressed that we could do high school math. He even recommended us to join math competitions and start a math club at school.

My friends and I get a 95% average in Mr. Barn's class. We do not like it when we score an 89% or less on tests. Whenever that happens, we beg Mr. Barns for a rewrite. Best of all, he lets us do that.

When other kids struggle in certain questions, such as fractions, geometry, and algebra, they come to me and my friends for help during class and after school. After we started helping them, their grades went from 60's to 80's.

Mr. Barns lets me and my other math friends do difficult math because we find Grade 8 math too easy. After we worked on trig, we started working on graphing linear equations. We know that the general equation of a linear equation is $y = mx+b$. M is the slope and B is the Y intercept. All the other kids get confused when they see this equation. When we showed Mr. Barns what we knew, he praised us.

"Wow, that's pretty high level math for an eighth grader. I'm very proud of my little math children,? he praised.

He watch us graph equations like $y = 3x+2$, $y = -2x+1$, and so on. Other kids looked at us confused.

In November, Mrs. Klein would always tell me and my math friends to give our math books to her. We had no choice but to. During the middle of silent reading, John and I went to Mr. Barns's classroom and told him what happened again. We begged him to give us some back up math work sheets. He kindly gave us an old high school math book that was published in the year 2000. It was still in good condition. We thanked Mr. Barns and went back to Language Arts class. John and I hid the math book in my back pack before entering Mrs. Klein's class. When we entered, she questioned us where we went. We lied to her about Mr. Barns needing to see us about our grades. We didn't want her to know what really happened because we didn't want her taking away the math book that he gave us.

Worse of all, Mrs. Klein gave my friends and I a half hour detention just for doing math in her class. That was not fair. After the detention was over, we went to Mr. Barns and sobbed. He tried to comfort us and offered to stick up for us whenever Mrs. Klein tried to take away our math books again. Finally, he managed to go with us to talk to Mrs. Klein. He told her not to ever take away our math books and let us have them. He also told her to let us do math whenever we are not in Language art's class or if we are done our language arts homework. Surprisingly, Mrs. Klein agreed. So, from now on, we never had to have our math books taken away again.

Next year, my friends and I are transferring to pre-AP. I can not wait because we find the regular curriculum too easy and we need to be challenged. I sure can't wait to take AP when I go to high school

Obsession with Physics

"James, what are you doing?" a tall kid asked me in science class.
"I'm doing physics."
"What is physics?" he asked.
I explained to him that physics is the study of motion and forces. I demonstrated by dropping my quarter on the ground.
"See, did you notice the coin falling to the ground?" I ask.
"Yes. I know that it's because of gravity." the kid said.
"Exactly. Gravity is a force acting on the quarter."
When my science teacher, Mrs. Bell walked towards me, she nicely told me to focus on the Grade 8 science curriculum.
"But Mrs. Bell, I want to do physics. Grade 8 science is too easy. I already know this stuff.," I said to Mrs. Bell. "Besides, I am at a 95% in this class."
After I did all the Grade 8 science work, I texted John, Allen, and Liz to meet me at lunch to do physics. I was so bored. I did kinematics questions until the bell rang for lunch. During lunch time, John was stuck on one of the kinematics questions.
"Does anyone know how to do questions that asks us to find the initial velocity?"
"I do," said Liz.
Liz and I began to write down our formula for the initial velocity and our solutions. We show John how to get the answers. We all grabbed our scientific calculators and punched in our calculations. We than checked the solutions at the back of the physics work book to make sure that our answers were correct.
"Guys, I got the same answer as you did, but I rounded wrong. I have trouble with SigDigs," said John.
I began to explain to John what SigDigs were until he got it. I explained that leading zeroes did not count as SigDigs.
"What about the zeros after the decimal?" asked John.
"Well," I explained. "You want to count those zeroes as your SigDigs. For example: 1.00 is three SigDigs."
Thanks James," Said John.
"No problem," I said.
As we continued to do physics, other kids stared at us and said, "Little professors, lunch is for eating, not doing physics."
We put our physics book away so that kids would not stare at us. We ate our lunches as fast as we could before heading to gym class.
During gym, we played basketball for the whole class. That was fun. My gym teacher, Mr. Ross is fun. He always tries to make gym fun, but encourages competition. In his gym class, time seems to pass by too fast.
When it was time to go to Mrs. Klein's English class, John, Liz, and I had to hide our physics books and scientific calculators. She hates physics as much as she hates math. One time, she tore up our physics calculations. We were so mad because we had to redo the questions again after school. On the next day, we told Mr. Barns and Mrs. Bell what happened.
"My poor little professors," said Mr. Barns.

Mrs. Bell looked at the three of us with a confused look on her face. She was also concerned about us because she felt like we were not focusing on the stuff that she was teaching. Again, I explained to her that she needed to let us do physics because we needed to be challenged.

"Okay, I have copies of your report cards from last year," said Mrs. Bell as she looked on the computer at our grades. "Yes, you guys are definitely sitting at a 90% average. I recommend you transfer to Pre-AP in Grade 9. You guys can do physics after you finish your Grade 8 material for now."

Thanks Mrs. Bell," said John. "You are the best."

"And remember, you can do difficult math all you want in my math class," Mr. Barns said.

In our Grade 9 year, we were in Pre-AP. I like it so far because it's more challenging. The studies are at least a grade higher than Grade 9. So far, Grade 9 is great, but I'm not looking forward to taking English and social for all three years of high school. Unfortunately, I need English and Social for Grade ten, eleven, and twelve in order to get my Alberta high school diploma. However, I'm excited to take AP math, Physics, and chemistry.

Dissection
by Thomas Nguyen

Robert: Yuck, do you know what we have to do in Biology class tomorrow?
Amber: I know what you're talking about. We have to dissect a sheep's heart. I hate it to. It's so gross.
Robert: I know. Last year, I threw up after I had to dissect a frog.
Amber: I hear you. I fainted once in my biology lab. My boyfriend tried to make a ring out of the aorta and it was gross. I told him, "No thanks, I do not want an aorta for a ring."
Robert: Well,I heard of this software that allows us to virtually dissect things.
Amber: Cool.
Robert: Best of all, we can use this over and over again.
Amber: So does that mean that we don't have to worry about puking?
Robert: Yes.
Amber: Cool. i have the app on my IPad. I think it will help us overcome the fear of fainting in the biology lab too. (Robert grabs his IPad and opens an app.) See? We can dissect a brain virtually.
Amber: (Looking at the screen of Robert's IPad.) Cool, we can do this all day.
Robert: Exactly.
Amber: Does this app have a heart we can dissect?
Robert: Yes it does Amber. Let's get started so that we can be prepared to do a real dissection.
Amber: Good idea Robert.

Obsession with Math

by Thomas Nguyen

I love math

And I don't know where my life would be without it.

Math has been my favourite subject

And it will always be.

With my math studies,

I want to get a PhD

And become a math professor.

I used to stay up late doing math.

My math teachers would tell me to get proper rest.

I am so obsessed with math.

I even have π buttons and a π mug

Factoring

David: Sarah, I have trouble with factoring and I have a test on it in two days.
Sarah: What do you find difficult about factoring?
David: You see, I do not know how to get the two numbers that add up to the middle term and multiply up to a product. (David looks at a question from his text book.) See?
Sarah: (Looking at the question.) Oh okay. Do you know that to get the product, you multiply your A term by your C term. Also, you want to make sure that the two numbers have to give you the product and the sum. Your sum is the middle term.
David: So does the mean that my A term is 4, my B term is 9, and my C term is 5?
Sarah: Yes. In this case, you need two numbers that add up to 9 and give you a product of twenty.
David: I know, the two numbers are 4 and 5. They multiply to get the product of 20 and add up to 9.
Sarah: Yes. Now, what you want to do is split the middle terms. (Sarah shows David the solution on the board.) So, you would write this as $4x^2 + 4x + 5x +5$. Then, you would factor by grouping the terms. Look for a common factor in the first two terms. Then, Look for the common factor in the last two terms.
David: So, the first two terms have a common factor of 4x. So I take out the factor of 4x Is that right?
Sarah: Yes. (David writes down his solution as Sarah continues to help him.) Finally, your answer becomes $(x + 1)(4x + 5)$
David: Oh, okay. That makes sense. When I first looked at this question, I noticed that there was no common factor for the three terms. I knew I had to do product and sum next, but I had some hard time with it. Thanks for your help Sarah. I will let you know how the test went.
Sarah: No problem. What are good classmates for?

Passion for Physics
by Thomas Nguyen

Life with out physics
Is like being without food.
Physics is my life.

On Fractions
by Thomas Nguyen

Fractions are useful.
I do not like decimals.
They are less precise.

The beautiful Parabola
by Thomas Nguyen

The parabola
Is nice and symmetrical.
I like graphing it.

Trig Romance
by Thomas Nguyen

Hello cotangent.
I want to be your tangent.
Together, we're one.

A Dinner with Chemistry Geeks
by Thomas Nguyen

(There are three people sitting at a dinner table eating dinner. Brad looks at Jason.)
Brad: Hey Jason, would you like some sodium chloride on your fries?
Jason: Yes I would. Can you pleas pass me some?
Brad: Sure, here it is. (Brad passes Jason table salt.)
Jason: (Sprinkling the salt on the fries.) Thanks Brad, I love good old sodium chloride. It gives the fries flavour.
Brad: I know.
Trish: (Looking at Jason and Brad.) Oh snap, we're out of sucrose. My lemonade tastes too sour.
Jason: Why don't you add more glucose to your drink. You know sucrose is bad for you.
Trish: I know, but I am craving sucrose. I need to go to the store to get it.
Brad: I'll make you some fresh orange juice instead. You will not have to add any sucrose. I think that you will like it better than lemonade full of sucrose.
Trish: Fine, I will settle for your squeezed orange juice instead. I just wish that we did not run out of sucrose.
Brad: Oh Trish, when are you ever going to stop taking in sucrose? Sucrose is bad.
Trish: Well, so is sodium chloride, if you consume too much.
Jason: I'll tell you guys a story. My dad tried to make muffins once. He made them wrong. And you know what the funny thing is? They turned out flat. He forgot to add sodium bicarbonate. (Trish and Brad laugh.) I know! Right? I even told him that he couldn't make muffins without sodium bicarbonate. He didn't even know wha I meant.
Brad: So, did you have to tell him that sodium bicarbonate was baking soda?
Jason: Yes.
Trish: My dad is a chemistry professor, so he would know what you are talking about.
Jason: Cool.
Trish: One time, I told my dad that we ran out of H2O. He jus said to get it from the tap because he decided that he would not buy it bottled anymore. I don't like H2O from the tap. It tastes like chlorine.
Brad: Oh, I actually don't mind it at all. I get H2O from my tap at home everyday.
Trish: HeyJason, I'm thirsty. Can you please make my orange juice and add sucrose?
Jason: I will make your orange juice right now, but no sucrose. Sucrose is bad. (Jason get's ready to make the orange juice. He grabs a few oranges from the fridge.)

Polynomial
by Thomas Nguyen

Polynomials
Are always continuous.
They are nice to graph.

An Undefined Fraction
by Thomas Nguyen

The numerator:
My denominator,
Please do not be zero.
I do not want us to be an undefined fraction.
Being undefined is not fun
When you become zero.
It's impossible to divide by zero,
So I am kindly asking you to remain a non-zero value.

The denominator:
There are restrictions that will make me zero.
Wherever I am zero, there is a vertical asymptote.
If you and I become zero,
The fraction is indeterminate.
So we must take the limit.
I will try to remain a non-zero value
As long is the restrictions are not plugged into me.

Chemistry Love poem
by Thomas Nguyen

I want to be your base.
You will be my acid.
Together, our Ph will be neutral.
When something goes wrong
With your DNA replication,
I'll fix every base pare.
As a metal ion, I will give you some of my electrons
And we will become an ionic compound.

Embarrassing puberty Talk
by Thomas Nguyen
Scene 1

(Terra and Mom are in her bedroom.)
Terra: Mom, I woke up with blood on my underwear this morning and it was gross. I thought that I might have fell off my bike.
Mom: No Terra, you're having your first period. You're becoming a woman.
Terra: (Embarrassed.)) Why do I get my period mom?
Mom: One day, when you get older, you can decide to have kids. You have your period because every month, you will release one egg. If the egg is not fertilized, your lining of your uterus will shed.
Terra: So does this mean that I need to get my period in order to have babies?
Mom: Yes.
Terra: This is so embarrassing and I'm only eleven. Most of my friends don't have it yet.
Mom: Some girls get their periods your age or earlier while other girls get it later.
Terra: Mom, when did you get your first period?
Mom: Well, I was a late bloomer. I got mine at fourteen.

Scene 2

(Sam and Dad are in his bedroom.)
Sam: Dad, why is my voice getting deeper? Why am I growing facial hair?
Dad: Well son, you're becoming a man.
Sam: I don't even feel like a man! I'm still a kid!
Dad: Yes, but your body is physically maturing. Also, your body odour will smell really bad. Your private areas will start to enlarge and you will start having erections.
Sam: Does that also mean that I would have a growth spurt? I learned about it in health class at my school.
Dad: Yes son.
Sam: Will I get wet dreams? I heard that they're not fun.
Dad: Indeed they're not. You will get wet dreams. You'll wake up with your bed already wet and it's like you have wet it. It's not like you're peaing on your bed.
Sam: Am I going to produce sperm?
Dad: Yes you are.
Sam: Is sperm the stuff that a man uses to get a woman pregnant?
Dad: Yes son.
Sam: I learned about this in health class too.
Dad: Good for you.
Sam: I felt pretty embarrassed while my health teacher was talking about puberty. It feels awkward.
Dad: Puberty is a normal part of maturation. There's no need for you to be embarrassed.
Sam: What was puberty like for you Dad?
Dad: Well Sam, I remember my voice cracking, my first ejaculation, and my first erections. I remember waking up with my bed all wet.

Sam: Did it feel weird?

Dad: Yes it did. I also remember my sex drive increasing. The worst thing was shaving my facial hair and getting wet dreams.

Scene 3

(Mom and Terra are in the bathroom.)

Mom: Terra, I went to the store to buy some pads for you.

Terra: Thanks, I was almost out of them. I only packed about ten pads and I used eight of them in two days. My health teacher taught me how to put on a pad in health class and she encouraged me to practice doing it.

Mom: Oh, that's good to here. Did you know that some girls also use tampons?

Terra: My cousin, Nicol does. I saw them in her bathroom.

Mom: If you feel like it is too much of a pain to use pads, let me know and I can show you how to use tampons.

Terra: Thanks.

Mom: So how were your first two days of your period?

Terra: Not as bad as I thought.

Mom: Just let me know if you get cramps.

Scene 4

(Sam and Terra are at school.)

Sam: Hey Terra, did Mom start talking about puberty?

Terra: Yes she did. Did dad tell you about boy puberty?

Sam: Yes. I sure am not looking forward to shaving my beard.

Terra: Girl puberty sucks too.

Sam: It feels awkward. Doesn't it?

Terra: Yes it does. Mom told me that everyone goes through it and it's normal. It's just nature's way of turning our immature bodies into adult bodies. That was what she told me.

Sam: Dad told me the same thing. He even told me what it was like to go through puberty himself.

Terra: So did Mom.

Sam: Come on, let's get to class. (Sam and Terra get ready to go to class.)

I Love Physics
by Thomas Nguyen

Oh physics,
So interesting and full of theories.
I love how forces act on the objects.
I find NewTon's Laws so fascinating.
I love how they explain why an object remains at rest
And why it moves.
I love how physics explains
That energy can be changed
From one form to another.

Life without Math
by Thomas Nguyen

Life without math
will be miserable.
Go ahead and call me a big math brain.
Math is easier
Than social science.
Math is what I excel in.
It feels great to get the correct answer.
I love solving problems.

Trig Blues
by Thomas Nguyen

Alvin: Hey Ron, I have trouble with trig. The right triangle questions make me mad.
Ron: No problem, I'm really good at math. I will be able to help you. Just tell me where you're stuck.
Alvin: (passing Ron the math questions.) See? How do I know which trig ratio to use?
Ron: Well, it depends what information is given. In this case, you are given a hypotenuse of 8.3 m. The angle is 35°. You are asked to find the side adjacent to the angle.
Alvin: What do I use?
Ron: I want you to right down SOH CAH TOA. This helps me remember which trig ratio to use.
Alvin: Oh yes, I think my math teacher told me about it. The problem is that it's all jumbled up in my brain.
Ron: Not to worry Alvin. I'll right it down on the board. (Ron writes on the board as he talks.) SOH is sine theta is equal to opposite over hypotenuse. CAH is cos theta is equal to adjacent over hypotenuse. TOA is tan theta is equal to opposite over adjacent.
Alvin: So in this question, I have to find the adjacent side. Right?
Ron: Yes. What do you use now?
Alvin: I use CAH. So that is cos. Right?
Ron: Yes. To get the side by itself, multiply the hypotenuse by cos of 35°.
Alvin: Okay. (Alvin punches the calculation into the calculator.) The question tells me to round to the nearest hundredth. So my answer would be 6.70 m.
Ron: That's right. Do you know what to do if you are given a hypotenuse and angle and you have to find the opposite side?
Alvin: Oh right, I use SOH. So, I would have to use sine. I multiply the hypotenuse by sine theta to get the opposite side.
Ron: Right! You're getting the hang of it! What would you do if you were given the opposite side and angle and you have to find the hypotenuse?
Alvin: (Writing his solution down on paper.) So, I multiply both sides by the hypotenuse. Then, I divide both sides by sine theta to get the hypotenuse.
Ron: See, you got it now!
Alvin: Really?
Ron: i'm serious! You will do great on the test!

More Math Jokes
by Thomas Nguyen

1. One time, I went to math class. You would have guessed what happen to my math teacher's plant. It grew square roots.
2. My buddy, Patric and I are going to math camp all summer. I especially can't wait to cross Calculus lame. As my mom was helping us pack for camp, she told us, "Have fun, but no drinking and deriving."
3. What did the linear equation say to the quadratic equation? I love how both sides of you are mirror images of each other. Your symmetry is irresistible.
4. What did $y = \sin x$ say to $y = \cos x$? Please be my derivative.
5. What did negative three say to Pi? I wish that you would stop being so irrational.

Math Geeks Eating Pizza
by Thomas Nguyen

Tony: Hey, I just made pizza. Do you want any?
George: Yes pleas. Can you please cut my slice at an angle of pi over four radians?
Tony: What are you talking about? you're not making any sense.
George: Okay, can you cut me a medium slice pleas?
Tony: Sure. (Tony cuts George a slice of pizza and hands it to George.) Thanks.
Jaden: So George, how do you feel about your trig mark?
George: I scored a ninety-five.
Jaden: Aw man, you beet me by fifteen percent!
George: There's always the next test.
Jaden: Hey George, who ever loses the next test owes the winner five bucks.
George: No way man, I don't gamble!
Jaden: What are you? Are you as irrational as pi?
George: No I'm not. I just don't think betting is cool.
Jaden: Oh come on, don't be such a zero!
George: I'll just eat my pizza slice before it get's cold. Then, we'll do some quadratic equations.
Tony: Guys, no more math talk please! I can't stand math nerds!
Jaden: Well, you'll just have to go somewhere else because we will be talking about quadratic equations.
Tony: Oh man, quadratic equations make my head explode! Just enjoy the pizza and no math talk!

Physics Haiku
by Thomas Nguyen

Physics is great.
Full of math and some theories.
It is my passion.

Chemistry Haiku
by Thomas Nguyen

If we break up now,
I will give up H2O.
Don't break up with me.

Chemistry Haiku II
by Thomas Nguyen

Why would you give up
H_2O for breaking up?
I think you're crazy.

Biology Haiku
by Thomas Nguyen

Biology is
very interesting and plus,
We learn about life.

Calculus Haiku
by Thomas Nguyen

I love calculus.
I find derivatives cool.
We can graph with them.

Fractions are Friends
by Thomas Nguyen

Fractions are my friends
Decimals are not so fun.
They are less precise.

A negative Balance
by Thomas Nguyen

(Dan is at a bank. Troy is the teller.)
Troy: Hello, this is troy. How may I help you?
Dan: Hello, my name is Dan and it turns out that I can't use my account. It's put on hold.
Troy: Do you have your access card?
Dan: Yes. (Dan takes out his debit card from his wallet. He inserts it into the debit machine and enters his Pin.)
Troy: Hey Dan, I have something to tell you.
Dan: What is it?
Troy: You have a balance of negative five thousand dollars in your bank account.
Dan: Should I be concerned?
Troy: Yes you should. A negative balance is not so good. Apparently, this means you owe the bank money.
Dan: (Freaking out.) Man, this never happened to me before! I am not too sure how I ended up owing the bank money!
Troy: When i look at your transaction history, you deposited a cheque of nine thousand dollars. Then, you ended up wiring money over to some business that claims to be a charity. When the bank tried to process the cheque, it turned out that the cheque was fraud.
Dan: Does this look like I've been scammed.
Troy: Yes Dan. You can face liability charges if you fall for such scams.
Dan: This all started when I was trying to sell my 1990 car for four thousand dollars. A customer offered to buy it. Three weeks later, I got a cheque in the mail and it was written for more than what I was asking for. The customer had told me that once I received the payment, they wanted me to deduct my price from the cheque. Then, they wanted me to wire money to some orphanage.
Troy: When you get emails like this and you receive a cheque for more than you are asking for, it is most likely a scam. This type of scam is called "the overpayment scam".
Dan: I wish that I did not make such a mistake. I was so stupid and naive to fall for this.
Troy: Unfortunately, you are in trouble until you pay the bank the money back. Wire transfers are difficult to trace. Once you wire that money, the scammer has it.
Dan: Oh no, I can't believe that I just did that! Why do scammers do the overpayment scam Troy?
Troy: This is because scammers want to wipe your bank account clean. They want to steal your money.
Dan: Oh shoot! I could I make such a big mistake trusting this customer?

Ten out of Ten

(Dedicated to Rod Rash)

by Thomas Nguyen

Verse 1:

Thank you for helping me in Physics whenever I messed up

And encouraging me to problem solve.

Thanks to you, I don't have any problems with manipulating formulas.

You were always helpful

And available whenever I needed your help.

You always encouraged me to figure things out,

Wen ever I solved a physics problems

By giving me helpful hints

And asking me how I would solve it.

Chorus:

Hey Rod,

You're my Quadratic Formula; I'm your Discriminant.

I will really miss you,

Because you are such an amazing instructor.

I guess we'll have to go our separate paths now and move on.

It will be so different without you

Because I won't have you anymore.

But I will always remember you,

until the end of my time.

Verse 2:

You are such a good Math teacher,

and you explained it in a way I would understand.

It was a pleasure participating in your class

By answering any questions you ask.

You made the lecture so interactive and engaging.

Your explanations were simple and straightforward.

I would get the concepts so easily.

Chorus:

Hey Rod,

You're my Quadratic Formula; I'm your Discriminant.

I will really miss you,

Because you are such an amazing instructor.

I guess we'll have to go our separate ways and move on.

It would be so different without you,

Because I won't have you anymore.

But I will always remember you,

Until the end of my time.

Ending:

What can I say?

You're a ten out of ten!!

Calculus

by Thomas Nguyen

Calculus is so fun.

I love calculus.

I sure enjoy taking derivatives of functions,

And also antiderivatives.

Taking the limit of functions was interesting.

I don't know what I would do without calculus.

Thanks to calculus, I can graph more complex functions

By determining the horizontal asymptotes

Using the limit going to infinity.

I can also use the second derivative

To determine concavity

And the first derivative to determine

Where the function increases and decreases.

I enjoy doing integrals

Using the substitution rule,

Area interpretation

And taking the antiderivative.

Calculus is fun.

π Day

by Thomas Nguyen

Guess what, it's π Day. I'm so excited because I get to recite π. I can memorize over fifty decimal places of π. my math teacher, Mr. Barns is organizing a competition for people to memorize as many digits of π as possible. Only John, Allen, Liz and I signed up for the π Day competition. No other kids wanted to do it because they did not want to associate with math nerds or little professors. My friends and I felt left out because no other kid wanted to join the competition.

The prize for memorizing the most digits of π gets a pie. That's great because I love the food pie almost as much as the mathematical π. "So James, I started memorizing a lot of digits of π a month ago," said John. "I can memorize up to over a hundred digits."

"Cool,' I said.

"Let's hear it," said Liz.

So John began to recite.

"3.14159265358979323846264338327950288419…"

John kept reciting π until it was time to go to math class. In math, he would show off to Mr. Barns how many digits he could memorize. Liz and I also showed Mr. Barns how much we recited π too. However, John knew the most digits of π out of all of us. We wanted to see if we could beat John.

Allen, Liz, and I spent all lunch trying to memorize more digits of π, but it was not even close to the mount of digits that John could recite. What were we going to do now? How were we going to beat John?

During the competition, I memorized the first fifty digits of π correctly. Then, I messed up from the fifty-first digit on and can only get up to the fifty-fifth digit. My two other friends, Allen and liz also struggled after the fifty-first digit. When it was John's turn to recite, he kept going non-stop for five minutes. He went up to over one hundred digits. At least over one hundred by fifty digits. When the competition was over, he won the pie. It was a big pie with a diameter of thirty-five cm. We knew because John and I used a measuring tape to measure the diameter.

John was nice enough to share the pie with Liz, Allen, and me because he didn't want to have it all to himself. After school, we cut the pie into quarters and finished it. It was the best pie we ever had. Next year, I want to beat John in the π Day competition. Hopefully, I will be able to memorize π as much as him.

System of Equations

by Thomas Nguyen

Solving a system of equations

Is interesting

Because you get to find where they intercept.

Best of all, it is much more interesting than solving fore a variable

In one single equation.

We can solve by graphing,

But best of all,

We can solve them using algebra.

A system of two equations,

Can consist of two linear equations,

A quadratic equation and linear equation,

Or two quadratic equations.

Teach Me How to Factor

by Thomas Nguyen

Please,

Can you teach me how to factor?

I need to know this for precalculus

Especially when I have to solve quadratic equations.

If I know how to factor,

Quadratic equations will be a breeze.

Linear Equations

by Thomas Nguyen

Graphing linear eequations

Is so easy.

You just need the slope

and Y intercept to graph them.

A linear equation

Can have a positive slope.

It can also have a negative slope.

The slope can be zero or undefined.

A system of two linear equations

Can have one solution,

Two solutions,

Infinite solutions,

Or non at all.

Linear equations with the same slope and different Y intercepts

Will never meet.

Because they are parallel to each other.

Perpendicular linear equations will intercept

At a 90° angle.

Two equations that have the same line

Will have infinite solutions.

Quadratic Equation

by Thomas Nguyen

Oh quadratic equation,

Your symmetry is so beautiful.

You are a parabola.

You are so fun to graph.

Your two halves

Are mirrors of each other.

You're one of my favourite

Equations to graph.

There are three possibilities.

You can have one X intercept,

Two of them

Or no X intercepts at all.

I can graph you using transformations.

Tangent and Cotangent

by Thomas Nguyen

Oh cotangent,

I am your tangent.

We are reciprocals of each other.

Multiplied together,

We equal to one.

Sine and cosecant are reciprocals of each other.

Cosine and secant are reciprocals of each other.

You are cosine over sine

While I am sine over cosine.

Our trig identities are reciprocals of each other.

However, my derivative is secant squared.

Your derivative is negative cosecant squared.

Our derivatives

Are derived

Using the quotient rule.

That's why your derivative is negative cosecant squared

And my derivative is secant squared.

Pi

by Thomas Nguyen

I am Pi.

I am approximately 3.14159.

I am the ratio

Of the circumference to the diameter.

I go on forever.

And my decimal places do not repeat themselves.

I have no pattern.

That is why I am an irrational number.

I cannot be expressed as a fraction.

If you are negative four,

Please do not insult me

Because of my irrationality.

Fraction Romance Haiku

by Thomas Nguyen

I'm asking you to

Be my denominator.

We'll be a fraction.

Fraction Romance Haiku II

by Thomas Nguyen

I would love to be

Your denominator and

Be part of a fraction.

Made in the USA
Columbia, SC
12 January 2018